Balancing Acts

Balancing Acts

New & Selected Poems

1993 – 2015

Yahia Lababidi

Press 53
Winston-Salem

Press 53, LLC
PO Box 30314
Winston-Salem, NC 27130

First Edition

Copyright © 2016 by Yahia Lababidi

THE SILVER CONCHO POETRY SERIES
editd by Pamela Uschuk and William Pitt Root

All rights reserved, including the right of reproduction in
whole or in part in any form. For permission, contact
publisher at Editor@Press53.com, or at the address above.

Cover design by Kevin Morgan Watson

Author Photo by Diana C. Restrepo

Printed on acid-free paper
ISBN 978-1-941209-37-0

*For Egypt,
the real and imaginary Home I carry in my heart*

Contents

Foreword by H.L. Hix	xiii
Words	3
What Do Animals Dream?	4
The Art of Storm-riding	6
Clouds	7
If	8
For Sylvia Plath	9
Dawning	10
Cairo	11
Hearts	12
You Again	13
Truth in Advertising	14
Undertow	15
St Sebastian	16
Taut	17
Which Will It Be?	18
Notebook	19
Since	20
Mountain Meditation	21
Hermetic	22
'Solitude and the Proximity to Infinite Things'	23
Desert Revisited	25
Colors	27
Dusk Scuttles	28
Impressions	29
Moment	31
Shadow Box	32
The Passing Fancy	34
Jeweled	35
Thin Air	36
Rejections	37

Dog Ideal	38
I Wept for Creation	41
Hard Days	43
Poet Try	44
Liberation	45
Homecoming	46
Skin	48
I Saw My Face	49
Alexandria	50
Loft	51
Intimate Strangers	52
Allegiances	53
Afterthought	54
Discarded People	55
Transportation	56
Thirty	57
Great Impatience	58
Interstices	59
Unentitled	60
Poy	61
Turning on the Faucet	62
Visceral	63
My North	64
Photographs	65
Short Eternities	66
Anatomy Lesson	67
E-café	68
Air and Sea Show	70
Fanciful Creators	71
Strange Fruit	72
Artists	73
Mystic, Misfit	74
Hotels	75
Flying	76
Drylands	77

Recovering	78
In Memoriam	79
Inheritance	80
The Day You Lose Your Fear	81
Learning to Pray	82
Ode to Spring	83
The Museum-going Cannibal	84
Shuttered Windows	85
Lessons in Bitterness	86
Mystery of Doors	87
Starlings	88
You'll Know	89
Inventory	90
Hunter and Hunted	91
I Googled You	92
Misread Signs	93
Hothouse	94
The Opposite of Virtue	95
Paranoia	97
Self-pity	98
Every Day	99
The Unclassifiables	100
Speaking American	101
Giddoo	103
What Is to Give Light	104
The Skin of Things	105
Ars Poetica	106
Taedium Vitae	107
For Rimbaud	108
For the Love of Fruit	109
Breath	110
Swithering	111
Poolside Epiphany	112
Stale Ale	113
Overheard	115

I-lashes	116
Here	117
Colombia	118
The Poet	119
Master and Servant	120
Pen Pal	121
Liberation Song	122
Circumstances	123
What If	124
Names	125
Dark Room	126
Alter Ego	127
Embracing, We Let Go	128
Step One	129
Exchanges	130
Kneeling in Stages	131
Choices	132
Egypt	133
Restless Spirit	134
Silencing	135
Lightly Breathing	136
Mama Ne'emat	137
Airborne	138
Night Bird	139
Tombstone Epiphany	140
Of Wicks	141
Endurance	142
Forgiveness	143
Open Letter to Israel	144
Crimes of Conscience	146
Hope	147
Becoming	148
Ancestors	149
What the Sunset Said	150
The Balance	151

Arrivals	152
Aging	153
Mysteries	154
Genres	155
Resting Place	156
Destinations	157
Ramadan	158
Encounter	159
Diagnosis	160
Eros and Thanatos	161
Protection	162
Gestation	163
Shifting Gears	164
Color-coded	165
Start, Again	166
Source	167
Prayer	168
Undertones	169
Fatal Attraction	170
Gradual Escape	171
Morning Stroll	172
Postponements	173
I Ran	174
Expedition	175
Voluntary Exile?	176
Acknowledgments	177
Author Biography	185

Foreword
by H.L. Hix

In at least one way, an attentive reader may experience poems as self-contained: they include within themselves instruction on how to read them.

Which means that a reader opening this, Yahia Lababidi's latest, most ambitious, most comprehensive collection, needs nothing from *me* to find pleasure and wisdom in his poems: they themselves give all the guidance one needs.

Here follows, then, a decalogue, not of things that *I* am telling *you* about these poems, but that *the poems* tell *us* about themselves.

1. They offer readers practice in the "art of storm-riding."

Even though, in "The Art of Storm-riding," Lababidi's speaker declares that "I still have not mastered that art" (but that instead "the weather catches me unawares"), his protestation does not preclude his condensing into this brief poem "the entire apparatus / of bearings or warning signals." As a parent need not be able himself to perform on the uneven parallel bars to help his daughter acquire the necessary skills, so the speaker of the poem need not be able to do himself what he can make the poem do for us.

2. They are "unpinpointable thought forms."

The poem that immediately follows "The Art of Storm-riding" continues that poem's attention to the sublimity of the sky, but this time the clouds are not ominous bearers of the prior poem's storm. Instead, they act as meditative "filters of reality," assuming their various shapes freely and endlessly. Lababidi's poems, like the clouds they observe, filter reality as they shape and reshape themselves. They do their work quietly, but only the most careless reader would be lulled to inattention, since we know from so many other contexts how often quietness represents strength.

3. They create a "fragile filigree."

In "Which will it be?," the poet asks, "will the fragile filigree that persists of me / suffice to constitute what was an entirety?" The poems may not be the poet himself, but they are what persists of him, a "fragile filigree," something so delicate and wisplike that it seems a spirit when compared with anything material, and seems material when compared with anything spiritual. The poem inhabits both worlds, material and immaterial alike, and mediates between them, carrying the material across into the immaterial and the immaterial back into the material.

4. They are inhabited by "stray spirits and ghosts."

As Lababidi has "Moment" say, these poems are "dense / with stray spirits and ghosts." Whether one takes those ghosts literally or figuratively, the denseness of their population points to how *animated* these poems are, how intent on what the poem later calls "inner processes / and conversations." This matters because we experience poetry not only when, in Emily Dickinson's famous formulation, "I feel physically as if the *top of my head* were taken off," but also when we feel spiritual presences before, around, and within us.

5. They refuse "false divisions."

We all of us know to suspect binaries, oversimplified divisions of the complex reality in which we live, but they are hard to avoid in practice. Popular culture presents us with them constantly, and they keep themselves conveniently available for our use. One of the tasks of poetry is to reflect on binaries, to resist oversimplification by means of them, to reject false dilemmas. Lababidi's poems hew to this poetic task, especially (as noted in "Dog Ideal,") in regard to "false divisions / among mind/body/soul," but in regard to other false divisions as well.

6. They heed "the vulnerability of all Things."

Lababidi's poem "I Wept for Creation" includes an admonishment to the reader to "Tread lightly, heed the tenderness, / the vulnerability of all Things." The poems take their own advice. Not only do they attend to things that are clearly vulnerable (such as the "dark dew-speckled rose" in "Swithering"); they also see the vulnerability in what pretends to invulnerability (as when he registers as "inner tremors" the flap of Egypt's "giant wing").

7. They inhabit—or are—"short eternities."

One of Lababidi's poems begins: "I have not found the key to myself / the one that will get the high gates / to swing wide open, and the lights / to come on, at once." Poems cannot remove from us our finitude, or remove us from our finitude. They cannot open wide the gateway into eternity, to make us godlike. They *can*, as Lababidi has the poem "Short eternities" say succinctly, permit us to "soul-gaze / for short eternities," to see one another *sub specie aeternitatis*, under the aspect of eternity.

8. They engage in "sweetly spirited protest."

The poem in which Lababidi introduces this phrase is an elegy, "In Memoriam," for a friend dying of stomach cancer, making "his last, graceful stand," and managing in the process "to give style to death." Like the dying friend, Lababidi's poems engage in sweetly spirited protest against the inevitabilities of the human condition, all the finitudes and failings, the *in*humanities to one another, and the losses that sum to what in another poem, "Undertow," he calls "the desperate fiction / of the moment."

9. They harmonize into "a soundless symphony, mysteriously conducted."

Aristotle observed that philosophy—the love of wisdom—begins in wonder, and nowhere is such wonder more vividly present in Lababidi's work than in his poem "Starlings." Often characterized as "junk birds," so common that we allow ourselves no interest in them, starlings seldom elicit wonder, but Lababidi sees through commonness to their "fluid arabesques across the stage of heaven / as they swarm and glide as though of one mind / a soundless symphony, mysteriously conducted."

10. They are "woven of whispers, murmurs and chants."

In the poem "Breath," Lababidi sees beneath "the intricate network of noise" a "still more persistent tapestry / woven of whispers, murmurs and chants" that is "the heaving breath of the very earth," the "prayer of all things." It is to that tapestry that these poems contribute. As prayers, they embrace all things: words, knots, bird footprints, clotheslines, orchids, matchsticks… Each is a whisper, or a murmur, or a chant; each offers "thanks and remembrance."

Balancing Acts

New & Selected Poems

1993 – 2015

Words

Words are like days:
coloring books or pickpockets,
signposts or scratching posts,
fakirs over hot coals.

Certain words must be earned
just as emotions are suffered
before they can be uttered
—clean as a kept promise.

Words as witnesses
testifying their truths
squalid or rarefied
inevitable, irrefutable.

But, words must not carry
more than they can
it's not good for their backs
or their reputations.

For, whether they dance alone
or with an invisible partner,
every word is a cosmos
dissolving the inarticulate.

What Do Animals Dream?

Do they dream of past lives and unlived dreams
unspeakably human or unimaginably bestial?

Do they struggle to catch in their slumber
what is too slippery for the fingers of day?

Are there subtle nocturnal intimations
to illuminate their undreaming hours?

Are they haunted by specters of regret
do they visit their dead in drowsy gratitude?

Or are they revisited by their crimes
transcribed in tantalizing hieroglyphs?

Do they retrace the outline of their wounds
or dream of transformation, instead?

Do they tug at obstinate knots
of inassimilable longings and thwarted strivings?

Are there agitations, upheavals, or mutinies
against their perceived selves or fate?

Are they free of strengths and weaknesses peculiar
to horse, deer, bird, goat, snake, lamb or lion?

Are they ever neither animal nor human
but creature and Being?

Do they have holy moments of understanding
in the very essence of their entity?

Do they experience their existence more fully
relieved of the burden of wakefulness?

Do they suspect, with poets, that all we see or seem
is but a dream within a dream?

Or is it merely a small dying
a little taste of nothingness that gathers in their
mouths?

The Art of Storm-riding

I could not decipher the living riddle of my body
put it to sleep when it hungered, and overfed it
when time came to dream

I nearly choked on the forked tongue of my spirit
between the real and the ideal, rejecting the one
and rejected by the other

I still have not mastered that art of storm-riding
without ears to apprehend howling winds
or eyes for rolling waves

Always the weather catches me unawares, baffled
by maps, compass, stars and the entire apparatus
of bearings or warning signals

Clutching at driftwood, eyes screwed shut, I tremble
hoping the unhinged night will pass and I remember
how once I shielded my flame.

Clouds

*To find the origin,
trace back the manifestations.*
—Tao

Between being and non-being
barely there
these sails of water, ice, air—

Indifferent drifters, wandering
high on freedom
of the homeless

Restlessly swithering
like ghosts, slithering through substance
in puffs and wisps

Lending an enchanting or ominous air
luminous or casting shadows,
ambivalent filters of reality

Bequeathing wreaths, or modesty
veils to great natural beauties
like mountain peaks

Sometimes simply hanging there
airborne abstract art
in plain view

Suspended animation
continually contorting:
great sky whales, now, horse drawn carriages

unpinpointable thought forms,
punctuating the endless sentence of the sky.

If

If there were more than one of me
I'd shave my head and grow my beard
I'd be a Doctor of Theology

In great coat of myth, impermeable to ridicule
I'd raise my voice and sing
hymns to the Unknown god

Another me would come undone, voluptuously
submit to possessions, deliriously
mate with night in vicious delight

I would be, in a word, unspeakable
indulge an appetite artistically criminal
gloriously indifferent to utter: *ruin*!

Yet another me might take to stage
part animal, part angel in improbable outfit
strike ecstatic pose, fuse with masses

Or perhaps, at last, renounce words and self
occupy an eye, to better see
in silent awe, peripherally

But, there is only this ambitious pen
and playpen, fencing a mass of miscarriages
trembling from time to time in unquiet blood

And I, with reluctant fidelity, am guardian
looking over the restless, violent lot
for fear of fratricide.

For Sylvia Plath

Sleepwalking, she prepared breakfast
for her still dreaming children, before
breaking fast, to satisfy her appetite

no fire needed, she all-consuming flame
bravely cowered on the kitchen floor
and slaked an antique thirst on vapor

laying her dream-tormented head to rest
took premature and belated leave, set
out to sea, having found no harbor here.

Dawning

There are hours when every thing creaks
when chairs stretch their arms, tables their legs
and closets crack their backs, incautiously

Fed up with the polite fantasy
of having to stay in one place
and stick to their stations

Humans too, at work, or in love
know such aches and growing pains
when inner furnishings defiantly shift

As decisively, and imperceptibly, as a continent
some thing will give, croak or come undone
so that everything else must be reconsidered

One restless dawn, unable to suppress the itch
of *wanderlust*, with a heavy door left ajar
semi-deliberately, and a new light teasing in

Some piece of immobility will finally quit
suddenly nimble on wooden limbs
as fast as a horse, fleeing the stable.

Cairo

I buried your face, someplace
by the side of the new road
so I would not trip over it
every morning or on evening strolls

still, I am helplessly drawn
to the scene of this crime
for fear of forgetting
the sum of your splendor

then, there's also the rain
that loosens the soil
to reveal a bewitching feature
awash with emotion

an eye, perhaps tender or
a pale, becalmed cheek
a mouth, tight with reproach or
lips pursed in a deathless smile

other times you are inscrutable
worse, is when I seem to lose you
and pick at the earth like a scab
frantic, and faithful, like a dog.

Hearts

We must not play with hearts
for who can calculate
what they are capable of,
or what they might become

How they slip, change shape
practice forgetfulness and purge,
surrendering pleasure with pain
as unsteady burdens of memory

Or how they grow wayward, wild
the wounded become wounding
and, in order to keep alive,
treacherous in the trenches

Until they are unrecognizable
to their owners, brokers or breakers
and what began as deception
proves to be a self-delusion

The heart has its treasons
that reason does not know—
why it must cheat, lie, even die
just to stand a chance at rebirth.

You Again

You again, of the singing wound
here again, lost and found and lost
trafficking in metaphysics and eternity
as the nearest hopes

where to, pilgrim
outdistancing chasms
rationing emotions
seeking sustenance

for the self too subtle and proud
for words
nocturnal flower, nurtured solitude
watered night

there you go, restraining the impulse
to say it all at once
even surrounded by silence
still filled with noise

now, having stirred some thrumming
hour when the moon throws
her full-bodied light
over all, like a silver screen night
of silent films, the whirring
of the reel.

Truth in Advertising

morning epiphany
applicable to love and life
in haiku-like purity:

only freshly squeezed
separation is natural
shake well to enjoy!

In fructose veritas.

Undertow

Then there are times when every thing pines
for the familiar pinch, that outgrown garment

like Tagore's caged bird unsure where to perch in the sky
disoriented by freedom and longing for the safety of bars

rather shame-faced, maimed, handicapped than pretend
to outdistance a past that is unappeasable presence

days when hollows ache, and the desperate fiction
of the moment can hardly persuade body or mind

or rainy weekends, when the heart prefers to curl up
replaying old movies, soothed by the rich melancholy

and drowning, voluptuously, in womb-like reassurance
of a warm bath, or the water-world of memories, dreams

scornful of good advice, blessings, and flotation devices
unreasoning, unseeing, ears sealed for all the din within

only to remember, in sober hours, there is no stepping back
into the same river twice, or homecoming for the Homeless.

St Sebastian

Sometimes, he found it difficult
to dislodge the arrows
preferring to keep them there
reverberating in silence
along with his invisible wounds.

Taut

between the real
and the Ideal,
rejecting the one
rejected by the Other.

rack of extremes,
the slightest touch
and I reverberate
awful music.

Which Will It Be?

Am I to be conjured by some image
happened upon in a drawer or folder

recalled by a dedication in an unread book
a cherished article of clothing, or trinket

O, great lover that you are,
composed of so many loves

what is it will summon me to you
which mannerism, phrasing, or view

what part of your mind-body-spirit
inviolably mine, as indelible as a tattoo

as he makes distinct claims upon your pulse
overtaking, effacing the footprints of memory

will the fragile filigree that persists of me
suffice to constitute what was an entirety?

Notebook

thoughts hesitate
to leave cave
sensing ambush

Since

I have lost my silences
I have lost my Voice…

peddling an Eternal currency
in life's bustling marketplace

irrepressible song springs up
and is strangled, unsung.

Mountain Meditation

Overbearing rock sculptures
carved from Time and Being
protruding, angular ribs
hardened, stony hearts.

Severe, austere beauty
bare, knotted musculature
intolerable masculinity.

Crooked, rotten giant teeth
a twisting sinister grin
old guards of the gods—
elephantine in girth, and remembrance.

The imperishable memory of the desert
craniums exposed, crumbling horribly
a rocky backbone, desert vertebrae
spinal scales of a sleeping monster.

School of inscrutable sphinxes
master storytellers sworn to secrecy
mute, pitiless witnesses, invincible
majestic grace and menace.

Hermetic

bearded black beetles
shuffle across sand—
ponderous, wondrous

ceremoniously, they smile
benign smiles, smiles without guile
men of the cloth, men in robes
men in dresses cut out of the night

exercises in restraint
exorcisms of the spirit
bodies without organs
organs without bodies.

'Solitude and the Proximity to Infinite Things'

The Desert is a cemetery
picking its teeth with bones
littered with brittle stones
marked by a grave air.

Mourning its myriad souls
it murmurs threnodies, while
winds scatter desert lament.

Guarded, hostile growths
defensive and aggressive
martyrs to their desert mother
they all wear crowns of thorns.

Tortured trees break desert skin
protruding stiff, bloodless veins
blades of grass, yellow and dry
shuffle from side to side, rigidly.

Wanderers travel to see and hear
Death-in-Life and Life-in-Death
To see Stillness, to hear Silence
Nothingness-punctuated-by-Space.

Pitting its stare against the Sun
the Desert returns it, pitiless
unblinking, exchanging secrets
of terrible, Eternal matters.

Indifferent, like Time, to time
resigned, without heart
proximity to infinite things
sets apart, makes remote.

Underfoot, twigs and rocks crumble
crack with ill humor and dry wit
taking perverse pleasure in pain
like one past suffering, yet bitter.

The desert has its dark jokes
over which it smiles alone,
Mirage is the word for desert humor.

Desert Revisited

under a whirling skirt of sky
streaming light and stars
groping for that tremendous hem
gingerly over quicksand

as though steadied
beneath some tongue and dissolving
not the absence of sound
but the presence of silence

or, as if transfixed
by a gaze, stern-serene
surveying a dream
foreign-familiar

incorruptible starting point
inviolable horizon
where eye and mind are free
to meditate perfection

there, begin to uncover
buried in dust and disinterest
the immutable letter
(first of the alphabet) *Alif*

under the ever watchful eye:
fearsome sun, forgiving moon
bless the magnificent hand
all else is blasphemy, a lie

experience quietude
the maturity of ecstasy
longing to utter
the unutterable name

only striving supreme or pure
can ever hope to endure
the absolute face
the awesome embrace.

Colors

Green is the color of a hope that is stubborn
White is the color of the hoped for oblivion

Yellow is the color of inspiration
Grey is the color of reconciliation

Blue is the color of a suffering subdued
Brown is the color of everything around.

Dusk Scuttles

dusk scuttles quietly
like a crab
imperceptible as eternity

the moon an ivory button
emerges gleaming
from the vast sky vest

waves like luminous cats
leap across
a dark jewel of a sea

dawn sands stand perforated
by bird footprints
in the shape of airplanes

Impressions

Misty and wet,
a low fog
hanging over
a still pond
in the early hours
of the morning

Subdued,
dew drops
on a black rose
dim light playing
on the back
of a dark jewel

Hazy,
lazy orbs
traveling
in vast space
twinkling
a stray star
from a far
universe

Glistening,
a piece of glass
a sliver of silver
sinking in a lake
of crude oil

Smoldering
softly, darkly
coal at the end
of a long night
dying

Flickering flames
the last stand
of a great blaze

Pleading proudly
and naked
but walking
not running
for shelter
Unblinking.

Moment

The mind is full
of elephants and mice
scuffling in corridors

the air is dense
with stray spirits and ghosts
swarming for soul

presence of mind
is to take leave of absence,
revel in necessary luxury
(an idle, perfect moment)

the balletic leap and twist
of a tremulous curtain or thought;
a shifting palette of light,
the lengthening of breath

or the secret thrill
of eavesdropping—
on inner processes
and conversations.

Shadow Box

the cinematic power in a drop of water
crashing against the stomach of a sink
smashing into iridescent pieces
scattering in resplendent shards

the torrid affair in the crease
of a week-old newspaper,
the tumbling creatures
in crumbling alabaster

unrealized populations materialize
undisguised before imperturbable eyes
creep in and out of a carpet pattern
once more irretrievable in the weave

come somber twilight hour
with its vanquished armies
a procession of angels, subdued
violent silver and violet diffused

a clandestine encounter
between a room and a candelabra
the four walls a shadow box
a profusion of unhinged imaginings

furtive fugitive figures
emboldened emerge
merge and converge
with a dark eloquence

a great whorl of specters
consecrating sacred pacts
enacting blasphemous acts
confidential, conspirational

monsters of darkness
huddled here or there
shoulders and knees
crammed in corners

the night, the night
with all its bewitching might
conduit for reveries
and gently taunting madness.

The Passing Fancy

The passing fancy of a gust of wind
flirtatiously lifts an evening dress.
At first, the dress demurely flutters
observing the rules of the dance, but

insistent advances capture its imagination
and it starts and trembles, exuberantly
shaking itself free of owner and partner
testing the limits of its airborne liberty.

Then, just like a thing possessed
a false note is struck, a misstep taken
and high above the whirling city
the dress is lifeless again, tangled in the clothesline.

Jeweled

Jeweled insect, ornate precise
drawn too near a liquid flame
trapped in a wide watery web
and beat its wings no more.

Fallen, formless crumpled
reborn on a human finger
first the glistening stem
peacock-green and blue.

Rubbing Death from eyes
set like stones
fluid and hard
with strokes geometrical.

A wing diaphanous
threads of gossamer
powdered glass and lace
catches color, brilliant.

Now, four fans unfurl
woven of air and light
beat in place, tremulous
take to glorious flight.

Thin Air

Thin hair
plastered back
barely covers
a skull more bird than human.

Thin skin
stretched taut
scarcely dresses
a torso more glass than flesh.

Gaunt, haunted face
all bone and hollow
tunnel eyes, little light.

Rejections

Rejections I receive, regularly
from the best and rest of them:

We have considered your proposal, but
decided not to accept it for publication.

Thank you for your submission,
sorry, we cannot make an offer.

We are unable to use your poetry
it is not quite appropriate for us.

We do appreciate your interest
good luck better luck best of luck.

Still I continue to draw and send forth
quivering arrows from this aching bow

Emboldened by Becket's wry quip
"Try again, fail again, fail better."

Citing Nietzsche's modest abundance
"an artist does not know what is finest in their garden"

As I arrange yet another bouquet
always, with Baudelaire, in search of the *New*.

Dog Ideal

without the need to stifle the cry of consciousness
through drink or drug or violent distraction,
disinclined to wreak havoc on self or other

free of the sustained illusion of written words
and images, with their enduring damage
or turning to the senseless spell of art for oblivion

their memories are not material
but perish at birth, still-born

always the present, unoppressed
by the burden of past or future
the unspoken and unspeakable

without the complication of human sophistication
or impossible longings beyond dog and dog world
they dream of food, shelter, air
and wake to find them there

without false divisions
among mind/body/soul
so without perversions

honest in their need to give and receive
a love neither tormented nor tormenting
nursing their wounds without meditation,
which is the creation of more suffering

a spirituality of the earth
a piety and humility that accepts
the man and God-given crumb
expects nothing

unconcerned with the pursuit of truth
and other lies
they live in Truth

never lost in the labyrinth of self
they are without self-image,
thus without self-deception

blissfully unaware of Schopenhauer's Pendulum
which from pain to boredom swings
their tails sway contentedly
always at home, in their bodies

nonchalantly, watching the world pass by
with benign curiosity and sideways glace
slipping in and out of untroubled sleep

they do not know the gloom
of deliberately darkened rooms
suspicions, fears and worries
real confounded with unfounded

or artificially purchased dreams
long after an inexhaustible mind
has exhausted its hapless frame

without question, they accept the deposits of Fate
without the added interest of personal doubts
questioning their place in the universe

unconcerned with peace, justice
and other human nonsense

impervious to the charm of philosophy or psychology
the conceit of thought, the paralysis of analysis
all idle speculation, and monstrous civilization

neither prisoners of Time
nor victims of temperament
without necessary occupations
or unnecessary preoccupations
with sanity

out of reach
out of reach
out of reach…

work like dog
live like a dog
die like a dog.

I Wept for Creation

A sandaled foot sinks into the sand,
and Time collapses.
The landscape is transfigured.
Every Thing Lives and is unfinished:
so much wet clay.

"Gently, brother, pray."
Tread lightly, heed the tenderness,
the vulnerability of all Things.

This is how I feel,
groans the earth
Experience my birth pangs,
witness my death throes.
Hear, now, the agony of perpetual creation
The earth heaves, breathes a sigh
the air is full of pregnant cries.

Watch the sky darken, hang heavy and low
with the lowering of a world-weary eyelid,
the vegetation, now, a deep matte velvet.
Widen the eyes, raise the head and spirit,
the greenery is radiant with light.

In the mystery of moods lies the mastery of scenery
with a look one can color the landscape.
With a look the parched throat of a canal dampens
wild flowers clamor to arrange themselves.
Surrendering her will, Nature is
transformed, formed, deformed.

The double helix of Existence
laughter-suffering
elaborately, they alternate.

Tugging at the spirit,
the side of the mouth,
the corner of an eye.

The tear like a pendulum,
swings.

Heart laid bare, mapped out
like overlapping tightropes
absorbing as a spider's net.
One misstep and one is caught,
carried away and helpless.

See faces contort, bend out of shape
the singular harmony of features
tortured by multiplicity,
violent winds agitating
the surface of still waters.

Ruins everywhere, rocks like bones
(as hard, as brittle)
now, age, wither.
Shuddering certainty where before
there was only intimation.

Safeguarding her Secret
Existence makes a mockery of words.
meaningless, words disperse
with a piercing glance.

Every Thing is born, suffers and perishes.
The belly of Being rumbles.
Eternity beckons.

Hard Days

These are the hard days
like uncrackable nuts
break your teeth trying.

Faces turned heavenward
pitiful little satellites
transmitting intolerable Longing.

Poet Try

set aside your imperiled existence
cowering before a heartless idea
prostrate before a hearthless ideal
spiritual asthmatic, straining for prophesy

verse versatile yet word weary
continue picking the teeth of things
loosening meaning with words, amid
writhing writing and growing pains

trust in longing to sing itself
ushering you to the horizon
of your hopes

Poet try

and endure
your Wisdom
gently mocking

Liberation

and, once you've arrived at the perimeters
of personality
that knot of contradictions, idiosyncrasies
called character
through the hall of mirrors
that comfort and distort

the liberation of undifferentiation
awaits the well-ventilated soul
pouring through open pores
what cannot be captured

you, brooding on boulder, shoulder
and impossible slope
yield to crushing truths
relinquish aches and muscles alike
relish the respite, and then return.

Homecoming

Crowded, unanchored mind
without moorings, spiritually adrift
citing irreconcilable differences
as reason for the inamicable split
in your splintered personality

Inhabitant of a separate intensity
adherent of an inner imperative
practitioner of a sedentary lie—
buried between the covers
of book and bed

Invalid physician,
nursing recurrent daydreams
recounting tall tales
like Shehrezade
to save your life

Playing with words
your only playmates
but diligently,
using words
to lose words

To sustain the gaze
for an eternal moment
to stir the reader
to poetry of feeling
excite finer centers
sound profounder depths

*

Having elevated the world
(and reduced it)
to Myth or Metaphor
escaping yourself in exasperation
returning with tremulous expectation
discovering yourself in everything
with wonder and terror, inextricable

Aligned with the bright intelligence of your blood
your position of authority rests in standing still
perched on the precipice of an abyss
in the indestructible and indescribable faith
that all this is mere apprenticeship
for the great promise: Homecoming.

Skin

Funny thing, skin
how it can make you feel
like you belong
to another or the world.

With its distinct instincts
memory and desire,
almost makes you wonder
who's wearing who?

I Saw My Face

I saw my face this morning
hovering at the base
of a coffee cup

eyes liquid black
and thirsting
lips parted as if

some great spoon
had stirred me to the depths
and left everything, swirling.

Alexandria

Balcony shutters flutter
secreting sea creatures
for an agitated cigarette
or a sensual smile

taking the air in outstretched arms
with open mouth
they drink the wild waking dream
of a shoreless sea.

Loft

Metaphysics
an exquisite tickle
or a joke
of cosmic proportions

Eternity
a homeless shelter
or a last refuge
of the failure

Hope
comes and goes,
you must change your life
before your life changes you

Intimate Strangers

Strange intimacies between unknowns
singular looks that affect us strangely:

the mute cries of souls in distress
glimpses into houses in disarray

searching, imploring regards
of existential curiosity

wells deep and guileless
clear to their very depths

or eyes untrained and unguarded
transmitting unbridled yearning
measuring our distances

those hissing glances
reeking corruption
drunken, reckless and thieving

or like twin stray stars
lost in some inner space
flashing an eerie light.

Allegiances

I am Destiny's son
loyal by his side
(I never wandered far)

Life is as remote to me
as Destiny is intimate:
an ache sweet and serene

When anxious, he gathers me in
promising otherworldly allure
outside all specificity

I honor him in all things
and he follows me everywhere
with eyes dark and tender

Surefooted and steady
threading through trees
I tread his black woods

In his night, I walk in light
in the dawning of understanding
and centered in his gravity.

Afterthought

and, when we pass are we caught
in the pockets of afterlife
——the sorted and unsorted——

or, do we continue slipping
through a fault in the lining
through the gaps in space?

Discarded People

Discarded people like plastic bottles
litter streets sidewalks and benches
out to air their cramped crumpled spirits
from rotting in long forgotten drawers
—staring intently at Nowhere, in particular.

Transportation

When beside yourself, blindfolded and bundled off
where all is winking confidences, suffused smiles
and a sense of imminent revelation
—a state as delineated as a planet—
here the mind's eye must no longer squint
for symbols embedded in the day

the trick is not to steal from this capital of riches
but to cultivate organs of appreciation
breathe the pregnant, wriggling air
acquire a taste for the return and
above all, remember the Way…

Thirty

Youth is passing, he said
with a deathless smile

It's tucked like a secret
in the folds of our flesh
it's written in the open
of our shifting features

Perhaps not in complete sentences, yet
a halting line here,
a faltering fragment there,
telling punctuation marks

Once, our blood sufficed as the stimulant of choice
hurtling through our veins, singing indestructibility.

Great Impatience

A great impatience ushers me to and fro
rises before me, and sends me to sleep
with anxious care

It matches my stride, heaving and sighing
while helplessly pacing or restlessly lying
in tense anticipation

Is mindful of me indifferent to the moment
amorously engaged or arranging the hours
like dreadful flowers

Whether swept up in literature's mighty wave
or wearily treading water with puny kicks
at the workplace.

Interstices

My hours are afraid of my days
mistrust placing their feet down
suspicious of finding a foothold
tic toc they tip toe, self-consciously

My days are afraid of my years
never able to forget themselves
standing around as I try to sleep
shifting their weight, shuffling fears

In the interstices, it is timeless
unwound and happily unfound
there we slip through the sieve
between those immeasurable spaces…

Unentitled

I have not found the key to myself
the one that will get the high gates
to swing wide open and the lights
to come on, at once

When not denied entrance entirely
I fumble in the dark and stumble
blindly, run into doors and walls
groping and hoping

I knock my head against false ceilings
and trip on traps I forgot to remember
then start at the sight of my reflection
bumping into myselves.

Poy

He plays with fire
up against the night sky
he looks like a man
juggling the stars

Now humbly bowing
harnessing elements
the chains mystically dissolve
only the graceful dance remains

Slow dancing the figure twirls
like a Sufi in a skirt of flame
or some spiritual bullfighter
with his twisting cape ablaze

Until amid luminous circus wheels
the flame ritual dies out
trailing a numinous light
like esoteric script across the sky.

Turning on the Faucet

What harrowing reproaches
from the depths delivered
with world historic accent

As though clearing a throat
spoiled by long use or disuse
to bewail an ancient crime

Cries of wrathful deities
growling hungry howls
of cavernous cravings

Or, strange pathos echoing
memory's dizzy playground
in plaintive desert threnody

Such sighs of fearful spirits in limbo
somehow unliving and undying
wandering in the land of shades

Startled from much dreamed of sleep
hollows aching, with arthritic creak
into reluctant and rusty service

What weird music from breathing flutes:
moving water, steel and air entreaties.
Oh, that sublime singing of the pipes!

Sublime in the sense Milton meant it
"the beauty that hath terror in it."

Visceral

The watering holes are contaminated
animals stagger, wounded and wounding
strangling fierce and bewildered keening—
there is word of a stranger in the village

spreading like lengthening shadows
spilling into once safe, sunlit spaces
splotchy-blotchy, blemishing news
as expected as a natural disaster

all is wet with fear of the unknown
sky and earth quake and thunder
before the hard truth of a reality:
the beloved has found another.

My North

Survival simplified to a difficult equation
under the dictate: overcome or perish,
transcendence has become a necessity

no time for tears or breathless incredulity
time to summon powers once bragged of
submit to be tested as man and superman

but first to adjust the compass settings
so that she who was guardian of my sanity
is no longer my North.

Photographs

A bouquet of expectations:
figures huddled and strung together
like a bunch of poignant flowers
propped up in an imaginary vase

Wishing to capture what is not theirs
to still Time's beating heart or steal
a frame from a still developing film
making faces into a two-way mirror

Already they gape into the future
at their own fossilized memories
crowded out the heart's album
and evaporating as vivid dreams

Unbidden like mental hiccups, they will arise
those frozen feeling-tone remembrances
whether jealously guarded in a chest of drawers
or happened upon on unguarded moments

Preserving what no longer is:
lost loves, illusions, or selves
they fill us with dumb wonder or dull ache
was that *really* me, and what have I *become*?

Short Eternities

… and when we soul-gaze
for short eternities it seems
her pupils dilate vastly,
become a universe
darkly gleaming—
to absorb you,
she says.

Anatomy Lesson

Like animals ritualistically gathered
helplessly mourning their dead,
museum-goers congregate to interrogate
flayed human cadavers

peeping toms and doubting Thomases
peek behind a curtain at secrets
usually reserved for physicians
or G_d

a tense dance of tendons and nerves
immaculate architecture of musculature and bone
skins peeled to expose gruesome-majestic fruit:
creation's inscrutable seed

transfixed, with car-wreck absorption
between life studies and *momento mori*
reverent, incredulous, implicated—we stand
mysteriously united.

E-cafe

a sea of disembodied heads
bob before life support machines
transmit and receive
rays of simulated reality

eyes glazed and opaque
staring out soul-less windows
will suddenly blink into feeling
registering unfathomable frequencies

sometimes making gentle clucking sounds
or abruptly ducking imaginary kicks
sometimes a fluttering hand will alight
on head, chin, or slightly parted lips

a gallery of caricatures drawn inches apart
hurried professor by harried housewife
nature enthusiast by flamboyantly defiant youth
loners, poseurs, punks and faux thugs

downloading bleak or enlivening news
their own or the world's, and playing games
with virtual combatants or unreal lovers
mating online, an illusion within an illusion

for an hour at a time, wholly alone, together
each utterly engaged in their life's minutiae
lost in private concerns, pleasure or pain
and the kaleidoscope of emotion in between

pensive, sly, delicate, expectant, impatient, forlorn
necks craning forward, scowling in consternation
chuckling, or glancing furtively over their shoulder
bodies undulating, and stealthily masturbating

traveling side by side, like passengers on a plane
though each in parallel planes of thought
racing in separate lanes, never *touching*
with nothing and everything in common

until time is up and they hastily disembark
with petulant or quickening step, disoriented
leaving hopes and secrets behind
in those inscrutable black boxes.

Air and Sea Show

The air is a storm of pitiless steel birds
the terrible beauty of fighter planes
mimicking natural flight formations
with unholy, and thunderous cries

Pirouetting and swooping awfully low
ruffling the feathers of real birds
and small children on the beach below
as they cower in stupefied awe

At times of an alleged war, on intelligence
there's no swallowing the bitter taste
of smoke, left by these flying guns—
these decorative killing machines

As they elegantly perforate an azure sky
with surgical precision and crude power
a frankly obscene display of military might
or the arrogance of shock and *aw, shucks*

What corruption of the freedom of flying
and the democratic innocence of amusement fairs
these screeching pterosaurs, branded "blue angels"
O, how they blaspheme . . .

Fanciful Creators

What fanciful creators we are:
bestowing *shock absorbers* on cars
sprinkling *tenderizer* on meats
and stitching *wrinkle-resistant* shirts

Such wishful thinking, this
giving away what we desire.

Strange Fruit

My dreams toss aside the sheets
like the skin off a fruit,
evidence of wrestling
with an invincible other

they make a mockery of taboo
effortlessly blaspheming
with blood baths and orgies
of diabolic intensity or rage

but all dreams are pagan masquerades
of animal deities, amalgams of persons
reconstituted, zoomorphically
hybrid monsters and angels

some visitors from the waking world
others residents of the dreaming one
with its own distinct time zone,
exchange rate, sites and tour guides

whence all this psychic flush
leaving us wet with exhaustion or pleasure
grinding our teeth to a fine salt
or mysteriously amused, with a half-smile

projections or premonitions,
these battlefields nightly revisited
to slay a dragon, save a princess
or, sometimes, vice versa

what of our role in these productions
glistening with irreducible symbolism
are we unconscious directors
or merely quivering screens?

Artists

Most artists are parasites
the way some orchids are
their independence a myth
tolerated by countless hosts

these climate-controlled hotheads
survive on generosity, indulgence
returning the favor with sweet entreaties
so long as they require these attentions

that they are ever forgiven
attests to the exquisite taste
of admirers, caretakers, and all
who shoulder the burden of Beauty.

Mystic, Misfit

These are the wandering years.

Born exile,
homeless at last
tormenting idea
become beckoning reality

Lover of longing's song
and whispered promises
all the colors once fixed
now, profusely bleed

Just as constellations disperse
the pattern no longer discernible
here, within reach, the future looms
high as imagination, deep as fear

Yes, these are the wandering years…

Hotels

Oh, the cheery melancholy
of those restless resthouses
half-way homes, away from home

Come, check into these dens
you patrons of boredom, lust
and pay-per-view entertainment

Such privileged inmates
showered simulated warmth
impatiently switching channels

You do not see yourselves
as the night does, shadows
in a flickering monster screen

Feverish with life, then dead still
each cell a pulsating peephole
to an unassuming dress rehearsal

A pitiable gallery of characters
pacing or seated, practicing lines
and fussing over their costumes

each absorbed on various stages
curtains partially drawn or illumined
actors eagerly peering through

onto an indifferent audience of trees
bare, and mapped out against the sky
like a nervous system

and snow flakes tumbling from above
as light and large as goose feathers
from a giant pillow fight.

Flying

Falling asleep is akin to flying
no feathers or flapping of wings required.
Dreaming is our natural state—
helpless sleepwalkers that we are—
if only we let it, envelop our days.

So, too, flight our birthright.
Mind and body long to soar
and were created to levitate,
all that is needed for this trick
is to overthrow our burdens.

Let drop to the ground with ponderous thud
what is serious, dense and weighs us down:
things like cares, worries, cumbersome hopes
so the hot air balloon of our spirit might lift
and travel light, indifferent to fear or longing.

Drylands

Tell me, have you found a sea
deep enough to swim in
deep enough to drown in

waters to engage you
distract you, keep you
from crossing to the other shore?

Recovering

Thinking, *about time*
crawling, through silence
slipping, past Yahia

In Memoriam

He preferred muted suits—
prison grey, mousey brown
before the death sentence

But illness changed his tastes
as though, dipped in terror,
he somehow acquired color

Blossomed in riotous patterns
sporting vests that grew bolder
as did the stomach cancer

The stealthy advance of blackness
brought forth a gleaming will
the bodily treachery, more trust

And that sweetly spirited protest
meant he smiled more, and softer
opening up as his body shut down

This was his last, graceful stand
emaciated and wasting away
in some way, to give style to death.

Inheritance

We inherit the things we abhor
the unsightly clunkers we scorned
and vowed to forsake as *décor*

Not the riveting paintings, or leather-bound classics
but the unwieldy, time-worn trunk with thick ankles
full of health records, half-truths, and debts to sort

Not the slender range of genuine strengths
but instead the absurdly denied handicaps:
the hunchback, clubfoot, glass eye, and wax hands

Not much of the enviable sunny disposition, or the amoral
anything-is-possible lassitude on parade before the guests
but stormy skies, sullen pride and tenderly incubated grudges

Hardly, the heroic public stances, more defeatist private habits
precious little of the extolled self discipline, gleaming courage
or magnanimity. In their place, a host of colossal smallnesses:

Chronic dissatisfaction, emotional blackmail, moral tyranny
self-pity, spite, dissimulation, tetchiness
that dreadful temper, this tedious rant…

And, to top it all, we must attempt the spiritual stunt
of not only trying to forgive the hapless progenitors
but their reflections that taunt us from polished surfaces.

The Day You Lose Your Fear

The day you lose your fear
of sleeplessness, you will sleep
and the day you lose your fear
of wakefulness, you will awake

Only then will you realize, my dear
'bribed defender of your fears'
that you do not need them so much
as they desperately need you

For you are far, far more than the sum
of these devious ciphers you suffer
the treasured lot clotting your chest
blocking an ever-rising sun from view

In light of their absence, you will clearly see
an essential self, free of borrowed shadow
you would hardly recognize that *you*, now
unflanked by those old fears… believe me.

Learning to Pray

Long susceptible to the pious heresies,
of mystics, martyrs and other fanatics
mad enough to confound themselves
with G_d, and declare it, free of ego

Those spiritually reckless creatures
contemptuous of all rule books,
traffic signs and speeding tickets
in such a hurry were they to arrive

No social drinkers, these revelers
they drank to get drunk, alone
that they might stay that way
-sobriety being the only sin...

But what of us without stamina
for such superhuman attention
or the patience to stand in line
inching towards the checkout

might we forge our own language
(until we can speak in tongues)
by asking of our every action
does this, or that, please You?

Ode to Spring

Momentous moment, when a great beauty
dons her bridal veil, stretches and blushes
in anticipation of the sensory feast ahead

When birds are restlessly atwitter, fanning
rumors of romance, budding in plain view
and making feverish voyeurs of all in sight

Having been buried alive in heavy virginal robes
time now, to try some color and bare some skin—
shy and bold, like all awakenings, and trembling

Pink, the color of blossoming, tender flames
cherry is the heady, sweetness of the scent
it's a wonder, really, that we all don't blush.

The Museum-going Cannibal

Upright specimen, looking to be fine-tuned
on weekends by the civilizing influence of beauty
standing still and reflecting in the refracted light
of another's encounter with the sublime

All polite smiles and hushed appreciation,
sidling up to some mounted painting and tilting
its head to sip and savor the brushstrokes, yet
downright vicious throughout the week

Hankering after a bit of meat and blood
in the shape of a live woman or a dead man
never mind, that they know them or not
at times any old body, warm or cold, will do

What a mixed bag of bones—when not frenzied
and teetering at the abyss of some bestial appetite,
turning around and donating blood to unknowns:
as charitable and vulnerable as a winged thing.

Shuttered Windows

To speak of the smell and feel
of books, the erotics of the text,
has begun to sound *perverse*

One by one, the old places of worship
churches, bookstores, Nature herself
become quaint and are vacated

In their stead a gleaming, ambitious screen
part shuttered window, part distorting mirror
full of wandering, restless spirits

Like so many ghosts in limbo—
free of the tyranny of bodies,
yet aching for their phantom limbs.

Lessons in Bitterness

Resentment is like drinking poison and hoping it will kill your enemies.
— Nelson Mandela

Some days it's especially hard not to think
the milk of human kindness has curdled
the same nights that all I could have said
ricochets in the echo chamber of my head

I'll replay alternate scenarios or conversations
letting my good friends and dear relations know
in a few unambiguous words, just how I truly feel:
'You're false, jealous and, yes, a spiritual vampire.'

Or, I'll read out my mounting laundry list of grievances
real and imagined, petty slights I pretended not to notice
Yet, I ruefully realize, that more and more of my affairs
are sorted in this state between fitful waking and dreaming

Until the ratio of fictitious exchanges outweighs
the sustaining, authentic communication I crave
and I wonder, before this metaphoric acid reflux
with its telltale regurgitation of all I've swallowed

Did I irritate my condition with undue expectations
or am I outdistancing past selves and associations?
Most likely both… but I also suspect this shedding
of itchy skin must conceal a nascent interiority.

Mystery of Doors

Every jammed door has its trick
how much pressure to apply
where to push, just so, how deep
at what angle to jiggle, pull out

So, too, with the apparently
difficult doors of opportunity
that stubbornly balk at all rattling
yet suddenly yield at the key moment.

Starlings

Hypnotic like a school of airborne fish
they frolic about in the open sky
flickering into focus and diffusing
back to the ether that spawned them

Gathering like a storm and breaking in waves
raining hard, a downpour of butterflies
flitting like a great kite, giddy it got away
yet guided by a steady and invisible hand

How do they know to spell such exalted shapes
fluid arabesques across the stage of heaven
as they swarm and glide as though of one mind
a soundless symphony, mysteriously conducted?

You'll Know

You'll know you've finally arrived when
you get to the point where you can leave
life's bustling marketplace, empty-handed

Smiling easily at merchants as they hawk their wares
of fruit and flesh, pausing here and there to admire
a fine raiment or strain of song, but not for overlong

You'll know you've cleared a hurdle and are home free
when you emerge at the end of that entrancing fair
unperturbed, without bulging pockets or hungry eyes

With absolutely nothing to show for the day's visit
but a small inner triumph that quietly manifests itself
in steadying stillness and a companionable aloneness.

Inventory

Here, I stand on the eve of thirty-six
mostly intact, and ever so slightly
more at ease in this twitching skin
(which begins to droop admittedly)

The manic fits of panic, exchanged
for unaccountable dance partners:
a dull, anesthetizing fatigue or
the relief of ebullient outbursts

Married, I who swore up and down, *never*
grateful for company, but still adjusting
to this, and all else, in the adult world
of professions, practicalities, money

My name I better recognize in print, now
to the title writer, poet even, I answer—
like a curious shoe, or antique brooch
that I wear out, less self-consciously

But, in this fretful heart, not much has changed
a human impersonator is how I feel
and I would not yearn for immortality
had I found a semblance of peace or home, here.

Hunter and Hunted

The work, whether employed or not
has been trying to remain
spiritually, creatively alive

Herding words, gathering world
spinning a wheel-shaped web
out of oneself, and waiting

To catch something of sustenance
wrap it in silk and ingest it
so that I might dream again.

I Googled You

To all those I dearly love,
but for the sake of my sanity
must avoid or cannot afford
to see in person, or even speak to:
Yes, I did, I *Googled* you.

Amid the shipwreck on the world wide waters
I found precious little flotsam bearing your name
a blurry picture here, some garbled voice there
still it was enough for me to summon you
create a history and sense of belonging

Of you, there is always far too much afloat
your smiling face like a cardboard cutout
that everybody poses with at the fair,
yet occasionally there will be a rare find
and I'll feel we spent an intimate afternoon

You, I check in with periodically,
your news and views surface in installments
that I rearrange to better remember
not how you are now but as I knew you then
when we laughed hard, and you were my heart's friend

All of you I miss as I trace your outlines
through the one-way mirror of my monitor
and when I shut down, you remain with me
as pulsing presence and murmurs in my blood
(thanks to that intravenous internet injection).

Misread Signs

False prophet, nightly heralding a man-made god
gilding the air with promise of revelation
a song, in truth, no less sweet for being counterfeit,
let us forgive the short-sighted visionary

Pity the poor bird its ill-timed enthusiasm,
its unholy lapse of judgment and misplaced hymn
having mistaken a common streetlamp
for the miracle of a rising sun…

Hothouse

I cannot bear
the perfumed air
of certain poets

where all is sweetness and verse
until someone dares to speak
without scenting their words, first.

The Opposite of Virtue

One might say, a vice is a vise
never mind if metal or moral,
it's basically the same device

with cunning moveable jaws
designed to fix us in place
and cheat us of a chance at grace

or like a metaphysical cat's paws
pinning down our spiritual tail
as we scurry freedom to no avail

Impervious to all advice, habit
hotly whispers false reassurance
while tightening its iron grip

It takes no effort to slip into vice,
but virtue is trickier to stick to
like the back of a bucking bronco.

*

There is never an instant's truce,
pronounced thorough Thoreau
between virtue and vice

But what of this instance
of the minor offender
with an innocuous moniker

'The Cuddler,' nicknamed for his weakness
of startling sleeping strangers
with his unasked-for affections

how odd his dozen or so victims
must have felt to awaken locked
in an elusive embrace of virtue and vice.

Paranoia

As heavy as a water-soaked heap of clothes
as subtle as four pairs of free-floating arms
undulating, pointing in different directions

one moment, a weightless independence
like a giant sheet of air-borne cling wrap
then desperately collapsing upon itself

suspecting foul play, how relentlessly it clings
suction cups all tingling with sensitivity
and wrapped up in a knot of dark imaginings

but, that's what three hearts and intelligence
will do to the emotional invertebrate
as they flee, hide and squeeze through tight spaces.

Self-pity

There's an X by my name
in some ineffable folder:
No peace for this one,
it says in the margins

In diabolical letters, I read:
Make him wait and suffer
wait and doubt and fret
let him pine for a short eternity

Then, a respite—he may catch his breath
(so we can toy with him a while longer)
Send a girl, a book and a day or two
when the open sky speaks to him alone

Here, the cunning instructions were in italics:
With stealth, steal a few key things back
sleep from his eyes, the smile on his lips
let his body betray him, his appetites torment

Turn those closest to him into ulcers
and weigh down his hands with Time
to brood, to doze, perchance to scream
in the midst of a pitiless afternoon

Should you fear we might lose him
shower the boy with small successes
(laced with the promise of defeat)
leaving him bewildered, hungering

[But we mustn't concern ourselves much
he's loyal, this one, and afraid to trust
He'll never leave our side, it plainly read
since he cannot imagine another lot.]

Every Day

Every day, regardless
of the night's previous
sulks or arguments,

morning climbs into bed
breathless as a child
eager to play.

Will you rise
in the same vein
to greet this challenge?

The Unclassifiables

At a round table they sat, called a truce
to discuss the indestructible world
and meditate upon eternal things

Like triplets, separated at birth
each possessed a portion of their truth
yet only made sense in unison

Tired of jockeying for position
addressing mind, body or spirit, alone
they came, like jealous gods, to save us

Unable to shirk their messianic callings
together they preached liberation,
through odes to joy and manuals of love

With myth and parable, the defiant muse
reminded us of the art of being present
and then how to vanish without a trace

More variations on the old themes: of exile,
homecoming, how to cut to the essence
of our humanity and unquenchable thirst

In the corner of a small bookshop, they convened
Philosophy, *Spirituality* and *Poetry*
temporarily reconciled to share their wisdoms.

Speaking American

> *O, it is excellent to have a giant's strength,*
> *But it is tyrannous to use it like a giant.*
>   – Shakespeare

I'm learning to speak American
(I thought I had it, ages ago)
but the dialects throw me off
each like a language in itself

There's the official tongue:
addressed to the better angels
of our nature, the huddled masses
all yearning to breathe free

But no one speaks such Shakespearean English
in the streets, there you are treated
to a more familiar manner of speech
the unguarded snarl known as slang

Unlike that poetic flourish on its tiptoes,
this dialect is flat-footed and suspicious
of the very tired and poor that it invites
preferring the right to bear arms in bars

Stray violence or casual hate of shifting shapes:
racial slur, ethnic insult or what specialists term
linguistic xenophobia…
you fill in the blanks, I'd rather not

I'm learning this fickle colossus
and the big friendly giant are one
so, if you want to run with either
best to watch both don't squash you

Having made a show of separating
church and state, they still *Bless you*
at every turn, but will also curse you
if you do not bless their troops in return.

Giddoo

I visit my grandfather quite often, lately
sometimes, he knows he is dead
and is almost apologetic for it
with a kind, sheepish look on his face

As if guilty of securing a reprieve
yet still grateful for a little more life
the way he was in his last days
treating every morning as a gift

Other times he's not sure himself
(as we tend to be about mortality)
and I suspect he's there to teach me
something to do with temperance

When he lived, and wanted to tease a little
with mock awe, he'd pronounce me a 'Philosopher'
a stoic of few, considered words, it was not for him
ponderous conversation or the big questions

In his last act, he was a humble man of the Book
which meant he found the echoes of my many books
(delivered in world historic accent, no less)
either amusing or frankly incomprehensible

For such talk, he reserved an arsenal of smiles
from the indulgent, to the gently sarcastic
hands folded neatly in his lap, legs almost braided
I'd tell him he resembled a human handkerchief

There are some, like Nietzsche, who take the noise
within, and send it out into the world, much amplified
Giddoo, as I called him, was un-Nietzschean that way,
he took the world din in, held it close, and hushed it.

What Is to Give Light

What is to give light must endure
burning, a man once said
Another man became the matchstick
that set a nation aflame

But fire, and its appetite, cannot be
calculated, like freedom
Injustice and desperation make men
combustible, like dry wood

When words lose their meaning
and an entire people their voice—
so they can neither laugh nor scream—
death and life begin to taste the same

From Tunisia, to Egypt, to Libya, to Yemen
the light from a burning man proved catching
And those with nothing to lose, or offer, but bodies
fanned the embers of their hopes into a blazing dream.

The Skin of Things

It should seem odd
to buy and sell flesh
for who can measure love or pain

Yet you can pick up just anything
for a bargain in the city—
quick fixes and hired company

What you don't bargain for
is the heartache, indigestion
or the hunger shortly after

The price of bloated pleasures
is delivered in installments
long after unwrapping a stranger

You see, there's nothing casual
about intimacy, or passing
through a temple, without bowing

Bodies are like poems, that way
only a fraction of their power
resides in the skin of things.

Ars Poetica

> *The mystics I like ... I like their ... their illogicality ... their burning illogicality – the flame ... the flame ... Which consumes all our filthy logic ...*
> — Beckett

Words in a poem are merely the tip of the iceberg,
the bulk of poetry belongs to a mass beneath the surface.
Invisible words trail the visible and give them force
just like printed paper, backed by gold, gains in value.

But, what can we do, we work with what we have
using the modest symbols we possess to speak
of that which we do not own. Like incantations,
certain combinations set a sentence or soul in motion.

It's the same with artists who use shadow to bring out light
or musicians who lend instruments their breath and limbs,
to summon music from thick air. So, too, with poets
who conjure hidden correspondences with letters

Which is to say, words only matter up to a certain point
(when you're using words to lose them). A poem is only
as good as the unseen poem it mirrors or, to tell it straight,
the Spirit that it harnesses and which swims through it.

Taedium Vitae

What's the difference, he quietly asks
between a death wish and life-weariness
or *taedium vitae*, as it was first uttered
in Latin, not too long ago, in 1759

By what name did it go, before that date
and, tell me, is it bitterness or wisdom
to surrender the gifts of youth, life itself
and say, thank you, enough is plenty

Must one wring the fruit utterly dry
or can we return the ticket half-used
no longer enamored by this glinting orb
or its ration of enchanting vanities?

For Rimbaud

Could it be that, from the start
the thing he sought, this demon-angel,
was always just outside the page

That, after swimming the length of the alphabet,
with fine gills and deranging senses, he created
an opening for others, but a trap for himself?

If so, then slipping through those watery bars
was imperative, a chastened mysticism—
and freedom to write in the air, to be human.

For the Love of Fruit

Winding through farmers' crates, the ladies seem torn
from *The Goblin Market*, an army of feverish Lauras

Dozens of eyelids, fingertips and nostrils agitated
testing hapless vegetables and fruit, like suitors

Pressing them, intently, for tenderness and endurance
bringing one close, pupils dilated, and inhaling profoundly

Rousing one woman, cheeks flushed, from her fructose trance
I clear my throat, and ask: So, what's the fragrance test?

'Ah, it's to find out if it smells like itself...
otherwise, it will be bland,' she sweetly smiles.

Breath

Beneath the intricate network of noise
there's a still more persistent tapestry
woven of whispers, murmurs and chants

It's the heaving breath of the very earth
carrying along the prayer of all things:
trees, ants, stones, creeks and mountains, alike

All giving silent thanks and remembrance
each moment, as a tug on a rosary bead
while we hurry past, heedless of the mysteries

And, yet, every secret *wants* to be told
every shy creature to approach and trust us
if we patiently listen, with all our senses.

Swithering

Sometimes, after the rain, returning home
the night is like a dark dew-speckled rose
and, somewhere, in between all that velvet
of those petals, we no longer are sure

How we got here or who'll greet us at the door
which indeterminate shape or tormenting love
will receive us with an embrace or ashen kiss
amid the mist and great potpourri of spirits

Will it be wife, mother, lover or yet another
shadow figure we've buried in a dream, or not yet met
such as the child who played hide and seek too well
long after everyone had moved on, into adulthood.

Poolside Epiphany

Stepping outside, it's not precisely sun we're after
or the illusion of perfect stillness, but something else
that has to do with the distant riot of children at play
stacatto squeals accompanied by the cawing of crows

Or the gentler song of slighter, winged creatures
circling above, frolicking, or pecking at the earth
while the patter of water offers its liquid paean,
and winds tease trees till they shudder with pleasure

This is the quiet pageant we longed to be part of
setting aside our book or papers to vaguely register
ourselves, easing into the pattern, our breath deepening
and our heart slow beating in unison with other things.

Stale Ale

> *If I write what I feel, it's to reduce the fever of feeling.*
> — Fernando Pessoa

I am only a pile of words
atop a stack of bones
stockpiling ink-pressions

I am also boneless shimmy
with finely estranging eyes
amassing devastating adjectives

I am only a pile of words
artificially propped up
on bounced reality checks

Gone deep self diving, again
hope bubbles break the surface
Hope, the window we turn to
when the living room turns on us

Or, according to old Kafkas's night vision:
hopes are merely mirages born of despair

Whittling away the hours

some daze better than others
time on my hands like blood

Hair today, gone tomorrow
these are the wily ways
of the pick-pocketing days

I am only a pile of words
sparkling whine
sacked in skin

Old habits hardly die
once bitten, twice sly

Weakened by the weekend
 still can hide, but can't run

How this must stink to high heaven
how the stench must upset
divine nostrils

Excavating gods
exhausting the patience of myth
clever nonsense, bloody pacifist!

Musn't mistake myself
for one who owns himself
I am only a pile of words.

Overheard

I have been lavishly gifted a pain
as thick and rich as oil paint

By pushing it around the page
I have learned to make Art.

I-lashes

Mind gnashing
for something substantial
to confidently sink
hungry teeth into

Mind lurching
searching for still
running waters
to cool hot hands in.

Here

We are here to remind each other
We are here to hear one another,
and to remind ourselves
We are here to remember.

Colombia

Here, in Medellin, what night lights—
like a resplendent necklace, glittering
against the bare throat of the mountains

Softly, coming in and out of focus
as though the mountains were breathing
between sharing a tender memory
of the city, with the valley and themselves.

The Poet

In the park, this morning, a boy
bespectacled, gangly, impish grin
idly chasing a squirrel with an acorn—
both proceed in crouches and pounces

Trailing behind them, a man
bespectacled, bearded, bemused
Armed with a tell-tale pen and notebook
the poet eavesdrops on youth and life.

Master and Servant

Rarely, having neglected his art
the man catches a glimpse of the artist

the cold, appraising gaze
that glint of an eye-tooth

better to turn away from the mirror
and best not to have a blade in hand.

Pen Pal

He went to bed, cradling a pen
his back turned to the woman

When he awoke, she was gone
and, in her place, a giant pen.

Liberation Song

For the eyeing of my scars, there is a charge.
— Sylvia Plath

He walks with a convict's gait
a dream-ravaged, slip of a man
formally summoned to confess
before a suspicious audience

He makes music with his chains
the one with wild, hunted eyes
disoriented and unaccustomed
to such confusion of light and sound

His throat burns so, he's uncertain
how he might find a voice to utter
his strange sin to the huddled faces
attending his trial and to every move

Then, a hush descends as he's introduced
by members of officialdom at a podium
and the crowd erupts into polite applause
for the invited poet at the reading.

Circumstances

The mind is full
of elephants and mice
scuffling in corridors

The air is dense
with stray spirits
swarming for soul

Heart like a spider's web
misstep, and one is caught
carried away, helpless.

What If

*If he truly believed in angels
they would appear*, I said in a dream
(of whom I spoke I can't recall)

Then I remember disintegrating
into hot tears as I realized
that I also spoke of myself

And in that wild, greedy moment
I challenged an angel to appear
as I cowered in a darkened closet

Full of longing and terror, I endured
the suspense of that great What If
—relieved the angel did not answer.

Names

To have a name and make a name is not the same
True, both are spun of love, and will and dreams
But one's blindly granted as we blink in the light,
The other we must forge from our innermost

Nameless, once more, we are reborn into the world
From the soul's furnace, we strive to stake our claim
Hotly hammering desires, giving shape to longing
And setting it to cool, approximating an ideal

Then again, we must teach this babe to crawl ahead
Mothering it with care, fathering it with courage
So that, one day it can freely live. apart from us
And find its place in our clamoring times and after.

Dark Room

Awoke, with an unseen
reel of dream film
I'd found wandering

And, now wondering
where does one develop
such unreal pictures?

Alter Ego

I wasn't meant for reality, but life came and found me.
— Fernando Pessoa

The first thing you noticed was how pale
the skin; the second, was how naked
a mess of long limbs, knees and elbows
you'd not have known what to make of it

The albino squirmed in the cruel sunlight
a thing of porcelain, as brittle and bright
grass scarcely covered the strange flesh
and birdsong masked its muffled cries

All day the dream-being remained that way
an odalisque of indeterminate sex
clearly in exquisite pain, yet alluring
and commanding an odd authority

Only when night fell did it make sense
(the androgynous specimen was male)
the way it crouched, danced and leapt
luminous in the moonlight, fearless.

Embracing, We Let Go

Perhaps, we are negotiating
not just with one, but always two
(who share the same soil, it is true)
one who lives, another who expires

A shift in balance begins to take place
once a love of silence is confessed
its roots run deep, its shade a world
and her fruits impossible to forget

From the first, we surrender something
and, gradually, consent to be emptied
transfixed by so much soundless music
drunk and sated through lipless mouths

What use to name this silent master
preparing us for dying or the Divine
—I'm not sure there is a difference—
but know, in embracing, we let go.

Step One

To regain our innocence we must surrender
our cherished degree in demonology
renounce all intimate familiarity
with those wily spirits of destruction.

In our defense against the howling
seductive entreaties of the night
we might clutch youth's mascots, and our love
fiercely against our trembling chest.

Exchanges

Don't grieve. Anything you lose comes round in another form.
— Rumi

What unexpected turns our losses take
in winding their way back into our arms:

an absent lover returns as many others,
a nation forsaken in the shape of a new life;

poems might take the place of mothers
and friends gone come back as a wife.

If Love were not always a step ahead
how would it ensure we kept up the chase?

Kneeling in Stages

Twenty years ago, a mighty spirit
whispered to me and rearranged my days
Drink, it said, of solitude; taste of silence
I did as told and it left me a writer

Now, it's back again with grander designs
to rewrite my soul or transform my being
Renounce, it insists, both word and world games
and I have no choice, but to submit and bow.

Choices

Two types of kisses,
and the choice is yours:
either with burning lips
that bind and blind,

or the lipless kind
always preparing us
to leave behind
a too-tight skin.

I stand helpless before
the sensuality of stretches,
but get down on bended knee
for the spiritual variety.

Egypt

You are the deep fissure in my sleep,
that hard reality underneath
a stack of soft-cushioning illusions.
Self-exiled, even after all these years
I remain your ever-adoring captive

I register as inner tremors
—across oceans and continents—
the flap of your giant wing, struggling
to be free and know I shall not rest until
your glorious metamorphosis is complete.

Restless Spirit

Pace, like a caged animal,
tense, in your skin prison—
and, when there's an opening
pounce, with all of your might!

Silencing

Most days, I don't read
or try to write, but sit
and let the air slip out
so I can slowly sink
to the ocean floor
and let the depths
have their way with me.

Lightly Breathing

The difference between letting go
and receiving, is but a fraction—
as though our hands were lightly breathing
first out, then in, and repeat again.

Mama Ne'emat

She loved this life with all her senses
regarded good fortune as ripe fruit
that she wished to squeeze and taste

She wished things were different, too:
craving a better education,
more independence and, at times,
to be dealt another hand of cards to play

Yet she understood more than most
matters one could not be schooled in—
say, the natural world or human nature

Her fierce independence of mind surpassed
women of her generation or background
"I'm worth a thousand men!" she declared

Now, my childhood friend and grandmother
has passed away, over eighty, she's free
to leave behind all that held her back.

Airborne

There are people you throw up in the air
who disappear, or remain there
(perhaps where they belong)
But most shortly return
and are heavier for it.

Night Bird

How night descends, enveloping us in its great sacred wings,
with the promise of a deeper silence than day dared to offer
Now, if only we can endure this tremulous stillness
we might still be restored to ourselves, once more

Tread lightly, cover the smiling mirrors and sullen screens
don't let any spirit escape through the 1,001 trap doors
Listen, those are your own footsteps you hear approaching

Don't look around, or move much, enemies of the holy hush
crouch nearby, ready to pounce. They want your attention
in pieces, smashed like a porcelain vase. The quiet majesty
of your mounting wholeness disturbs them more than anything else

Try, try with all your might, to make it last the night. As you tremble
and sweat, remember this triumph next time you forsake your oaths.

Tombstone Epitaph

Here, a monk and a satyr,
an ascetic and an aesthete,
did long and bloody battle
over a tender human heart.

Of Wicks

Silence is like a candle,
it must be carefully tended,
so that it does not sputter
and burns brightly, evenly.

Endurance

Don't squander your boredom,
dig deeper,
there are treasures buried there.

Forgiveness

And, when we pass,
perhaps we are forgiven,
if we are forgiven by all
whom we wronged, here.

Open Letter to Israel

> *He who fights monsters should see to it that, in the process, he does not become a monster.*
> *— Nietzsche*

Tell me, what steel entered your heart,
what fear made you rabid,
what hate drove out pity?

How could you forget
that how we fight a battle
determines who we become,
when did you grow reckless
with the state of your soul?

We are responsible for our enemy,
compassion is to consider the role
that we play in their creation.

If you prick us, do we not bleed?
… If you poison us, do we not die?
and if you wrong us, shall we not revenge?

Strange, how one hate enables another;
how they are like unconscious allies,
darkly united in blocking out the Light.

Yes, we can lend ideas our breath, but ideals—
Peace, Justice, Freedom—require our entire lives
and, all who are tormented by such ideals
must learn to make an ally of humility.

Truth, and conscience, can be like large, bothersome flies
—brush them away and they return, buzzing louder
nearly 2,000 dead, in Gaza, 500 children
no, these are unbearable casualties to ignore

To speak nothing of the intangible casualties:
damage done to our collective psyche, trust, and sleep
no more nightmares, please, give us back our dreams
we can still begin, again, and must
wisdom is a return to innocence.

Crimes of Conscience
for Snowden

Each time we betray our conscience,
we strangle an angel.
Yet, it's not at all certain
we're allotted an infinite supply
of these winged pardons.

Unheeded pricks of conscience
soon become soul-skewering
So that paradise seems a hell
and one must betray luxury,
safety and hearth to tell the truth

The only cowardice being silence
the only courage one's convictions;
and allegiance to a higher state,
the only chance at purifying grace.

Hope

Hope's not quite as it seems,
it's slimmer than you'd think
and less steady on its feet

Sometimes, it's out of breath
can hardly see ahead
and cries itself to sleep

It may not tell you all this
or the times it cheated death
but, if you knew it, you'd know

how Hope can keep a secret.

Becoming

He learned to write poetry
the elementary way
—one agonizing line or
liberating verse, at a time—
by *becoming* a poem.

Ancestors

Words seldom stand alone
like us, they are encircled
by spirits of their ancestors.

What the Sunset Said

Something happened as the light was dying
it wasn't just post-coital exhalation
where the once-possessed body is used up
and all that remains is bodiless trance

Rather, it seemed they were mirroring
a preternatural stillness,
two spiritual sentinels
transfixed and somehow Other

Science calls it "twilight calibrated magnetic compass"
yet it appeared beyond mere direction-finding
more a kind of existential orientation
consolidating all they knew, and listening

with their entire being, participating
silently, in a universal hymn
until they were pulled, as out of a viscous substance,
by the hungry cry of their nearby young

to become two feral pigeons, again
with this-world considerations
parenting, foraging, keeping alive
and, dazed, they consented to their stations.

The Balance

Hard, the poet tried
yet, much of the poetry
slipped the poem's net.

Arrivals

I don't quite know how it occurred
that this great fish has appeared
almost fully-formed, it seemed
to crowd out all else in my aquarium

Perhaps, this creature of the depths
always was, just out of sight
secretly feeding on hidden longing
and now demands acknowledging

With the swish of a majestic tail
it's upset my incidental decor—
gone the rubber diver and plastic treasure.
The glass frame itself can't be far behind . . .

Aging

I'm being hollowed out, I feel it
in the subtle droop of skin and will
Like the life stuffing were slowly
being spooned from me

My mind, too, is being emptied
of needless concerns
(such as, who's in charge)
traveling lighter, demanding less

One day, I'll finally slip out this
loosening body bag
Simply sling it over the shoulder
of my sturdy spirit.

Mysteries

I don't know the line
where prose ends
and poetry begins

Poetry, like the Divine,
will only answer our call
when there is no one
else for us to turn to.

Genres

I don't read books as much
I read more faces, now
scanning them for pity,
nobility or humility—
something to live by.

Resting Place

There are no maps for the land
my mind's eye is fixed upon
Instead a trail of wrecked ships
mark this treacherous path

My guide, a mysterious star
whose light dims if, briefly,
I happen to turn away—
and which glows brighter
when my heart's aflame.

Destinations

There are books, like experiences,
that measure our distances
and cannot be read until
we reach their remote shores.

Ramadan

month of quiet strength
and loud weaknesses

when our stubborn habits
and discarded resolutions

are re-examined under the regard
and rigorous slowness of fasting

testing our appetite
for transfiguration

month of waiting and wading
through the shallows to the Deep.

Encounter

I stirred in the small hours of the morning. Sensing a presence, I did not return to sleep, but ventured into the living room, apprehensively.
There, by the balcony, sat a familiar figure—cross-legged and reading in the semi-dark, with just the milky moonlight for company.
I do not know how I knew, but I did. I recognized the intruder, at once, with a mixture of dread and affection.
"I'm sorry," were the only words to leave my lips.
"I'm sorry, too," replied my longed-for-self, with a sense of infinite kindness and pity
He did not rise to greet me and, somehow, spoke without words, transmitting what was needed.

Catching his glistening eye, the caring made me cry.
"You've taken every detour to avoid me," he gently reproached.
"For every step I've taken towards you, you've taken two back."
I did not know what to say in my defense; how could I protest against myself?
"I missed you," he said, "and feared you'd forgotten me."
His admonishment was tender as a kiss.
"I visit from time to time, and hope you'll ask me to stay."
I knew what he said was true, and felt that way, too.
"I worried," he continued, "if I postponed this visit, we might never meet, in this life… and so I came to sharpen your appetite."
He rose and softly moved towards me.
"There's no need to speak, return to sleep. But when you rise, try to remember me. And to keep awake."

Diagnosis

If experiencing a feeling of general unease
that promptly returns as soon as it leaves
Perhaps it's not the case of a nagging flu
keeping you from enjoying what you used to
Consider this: the thing making you wince
might just be a newly-developing Conscience.

Eros and Thanatos

We live, love and create
as best as we can
but, sometimes, in haste
—lest we succumb
to the siren call
of self-destruction.

Protection

To guard yourself
against the evils
of this sad world,
keep your lips wet
with the sweet taste
of revelation.

Gestation

This long disorientation,
I, now, understand better;
as my soul is rewritten
I have been learning, again
how to walk and breathe
—under water and on air.

It's best not to say too much
or think you know anything;
preferable to keep very still
lest you might spoil it all
—when you are being reborn.

Gestation is hardly time
for any grand pronouncements:
lie low, feed and listen for clues.
Grow, inwardly, in knowing
before declaring it to the world.

Shifting Gears

Next time you find
the wheels of your mind
spinning (in vain)
think less, thank more.

Color-coded

To start with, saints are brown
like everything around
Then blue, from trying
the fine art of dying
At last, they're lavender
the color of surrender.

Start, Again

Sunset is a gentle master to all that are stricken
patiently, teaching us how to melt a bruise away
Watch how, with a silver whisk, that cracked egg
of a setting sun is majestically stirred, and put to rest.

Violent violet, pining pink, and yelling yellow
all agitated, then muted, their differences reconciled
until all that remains is a faint tattoo of quiet hurt
pearlescent wisps of smoke from a sighing flame

that night stealthily smothers and hushes away…

Source

Ear plugs and eye mask
are useless sleep aids
when noise and chaos
are on the inside.

Prayer

Books, as beads, on a rosary
tugging on one after the other
to be carried away to the vast
and then returned to safe harbor.

Undertones

Yes, we spoke,
but it's in silence
we understood.

O, translators of words,
think a hundred times before
attempting to interpret
the countless silences.

Fatal Attraction

Flitting by that oh-so-bright flame of fame
wings singed it returned, again and again
regretting it was not consumed—a *Name*!

Gradual Escape

In the mirror, old age is peering through
my features grow more distant, indistinct
—blurring the iron bars of personality.

Mourning Stroll

An old man, hobbling down the pavement
supported by crutches, pauses
before a noisy schoolyard
—children frolic in the sun

Through thick glasses and heavy hearing aid
he strains to see and hear, what...
but his own golden boyhood?
The eyes well up with easy tears.

Postponements

The child refusing to bathe,
preferring to play in mud,
is not unlike an adult
avoiding a cleansing
encounter with the Spirit.

I Ran

I ran hard and far
to outdistance my pain
But, when I got lost
my pain found me—
caressed me, wordlessly
and carried me Home.

Expedition

After decades of exploration,
discovering I stand at the shore
of intellectual knowledge
before an infinite sea
of the esoteric.

Voluntary Exile?

No matter how voluntary
it may appear,
exile is never
really a choice
—but banishment
from the land of the living.

Publication Credits

Grateful acknowledgement is extended to the publishers of two slim volumes of my poetry: Fever Dreams (Crisis Chronicles Press) and Barely There (Wipf and Stock) where some poems in this collection have appeared, in addition to the fine editors of journals/websites, listed below:

Achiote Press
    Anatomy Lesson

American Circus
    Egypt

a-Rab magazine, UC Berkeley
    Air and Sea Show

The Arab Review
    Swithering
    Ars Poetica
    Giddoo
    Overheard

The Art of Being Human (Switzerland)
    Passing Fancy
    Transportation
    Moment

Arts & Opinion
    Morning
    Liberation
    The Poet

Asia Writes (Philippines)
>Speaking American

Berfrois (UK)
>Embracing, We Let Go
>Liberation Song

Black Herald (France)
>"Solitude, and the Proximity to Infinite Things"

British Community Times (Egypt)
>Artists

Cimarron Review
>Words
>What Do Animals Dream?

Conversation Poetry Quarterly (UK)
>Shuttered Windows

Delmarva Review
>I Saw My Face

ditch (Canada)
>Poy

Dogs Singing : A Tribute Anthology (Salmon Poetry, Ireland)
>Dog Ideal

Dreamcatcher (UK)
>Hearts
>Which Will It Be?

Electronic Intifada (Palestine)
    Open Letter to Israel

Elephant Journal
    Breath
    Spirit
    Opposite of Virtue
    Kneeling in Stages

Eyewear Publishing (UK)
    Crimes of Conscience

Haight Ashbury Literary Journal
    Interstices

Happiness, The Delight-Tree: An Anthology of Contemporary International Poetry
    You'll Know

Idler & New Internationalist (UK)
    What is to Give Light

In Our Own Words – A Generation Defining Itself – Volume 8
    Afterthought

Invisible College Magazine
    Ode to Spring
    Turning on the Faucet
    Loft
    I Wept for Creation
    Inheritance
    Hunter and Hunted
    Photographs
    Why Marry

Publication Credits

IWA (Islamic Writer's Alliance) Award for Third Annual Poetry Contest
    Desert Revisited

Leviathan: Journal of Melville Studies
    The Art of Storm-riding
    Clouds
    If
    To Sylvia Plath
    Drylands

Liberated Muse, Volume II: Betrayal Wears a Pretty Face
    Self-pity
    Lessons in Bitterness

The Literati Quarterly
    Exchanges
    In Memoriam

The London Magazine (UK)
    What If

Mad Hatters' Review
    Shadow Box
    For Rimbaud

Mahmag World Literature
    Hope
    Circumstances
    Colombia

Mizna: Prose, Poetry and Art Exploring Arab America
    Cairo

The Monongahela Review
    Unentitled

Montreal Serai (Canada)
    E-café

Numéro Cinq
    Dark Room
    Alter Ego
    Pen Pal
    Master & Servant
    St. Sebastian

On Being with Krista Tippett
    Learning to Pray
    Encounter

Orbis (UK)
    You Again
    Truth in Advertising

Other Poetry (UK)
    Dawning

The Other Voices International Project Anthology
    Visceral

Poets Against War
    Hard Days

Prole (UK)
    I Googled You

Radius of Arab American Writers (RAWI)
    Fanciful Creators

Stranger at Home, Poetry Anthology (USA/Russia)
> Mystic, Misfit

Tell Me More (NPR)
> Spirit
> Reaching
> Hunter and Hunted

Thumbnail
> Hothouse
> Drylands

Tiferet
> Desert Revisited

Unrorean
> The Unclassifiables

World Literature Today
> Inventory
> Museum-going Cannibal

Zaporogue
> Starlings
> Mystery of Doors

SELECTED REPRINTS FROM ANTHOLOGIES AND FOREIGN NEWSPAPERS:

Ahram Weekly (Egypt)
> Cairo
> Hearts

Kuwait Times (Kuwait)
> Words
> Dawning
> Cairo

Literature: An Introduction to Reading and Writing
   (US College Textbook)
      What Do Animals Dream?

Literary World Review (Slovakia)
   Words
   Dawning

The Poet's Quest for God (UK Anthology)
   Breath

Silver Spring Voice
   Dawning
   I Googled You
   Shuttered Windows

YAHIA LABABIDI is an Egyptian-American thinker and poet, twice-nominated for a Pushcart Prize. His work appears in international publications and websites, such as: *AGNI, On Being, World Literature Today, The London Magazine, Philosophy Now* and *Rain Taxi*, while he has been featured on *NPR, Al Jazeera*, and in *The Guardian*, among other places.

Lababidi's first book *Signposts to Elsewhere* (Jane Street Press) was selected as a 2008 Book of the Year by *The Independent* (UK). His next book, the critically acclaimed collection of literary and cultural essays, *Trial by Ink: From Nietzsche to Belly-Dancing* was followed by a well-received poetry collection, *Fever Dreams*. Lababidi's latest books are a series of ecstatic, literary dialogues with Alex Stein, *The Artist as Mystic: Conversations with Yahia Lababidi*, as well as a collection of short poems, *Barely There*, touching on the life of the spirit. He was chosen as a Juror for the 2012 Neustadt International Prize for Literature.

Lababidi's work has also appeared in several anthologies, such as *Geary's Guide to the World's Great Aphorists*, where he is the only contemporary Arab poet featured; the best-selling US college textbook, *Literature: An Introduction to*

185

Reading and Writing; and, most recently, *Short Flights,* the first collection of modern American aphorists. His writing has been translated into several languages, including Arabic, Hebrew, French, German, Spanish, Slovak, Italian, and Dutch. Lababidi has participated in international poetry festivals in the United States, Eastern Europe, as well as the Middle East, while video adaptations of his poems have been shown in film festivals worldwide.